DATE DUE

DEMCO 38-296

CORPORAL
WORKS

LYNN DOMINA

FOUR WAY BOOKS
Marshfield

PS 3554 .O4619 C67 1995

Domina, Lynn.

Corporal works

Library of Congress Number 94 -71637

ISBN 1-884800-03-3

Cover Design Peter Fahrni
Design by Acme Art, Inc.
Manufactured in the United States of America

This book is printed on acid-free paper.

Four Way Books is a division of Friends of
Writers, Inc., a Vermont-based not-for-profit
corporation.

For Barb Domina

ACKNOWLEDGMENTS

The author wishes to thank the editors of the following magazines, in which these poems first appeared, occasionally in earlier versions:

American Literary Review: "Rowing toward Pine Island"

Ascent: "Habits of Grief," reprinted in *Anthology of Magazine Verse and Yearbook of American Poetry, 1986-87*

The Cimmaron Review: "Bats"

Gulf Stream: "The Pharaoh's Servant"

The Indiana Review: "The Olde World Cafe"

The Laurel Review: "White Candles," "A White Jug and Large White Bowl"

Memphis State Review: "With My Husband"

The Mid-American Review: "Dusk on the Lake"

Negative Capability: "Dancers at Rest"

The Northwest Review: "Taking Leave"

Ordinary Time: The Church and the Artist: "Lauds"

Oxford Magazine: "Sponge Bath," "The Orange"

Passages North: "Apples"

The Pennsylvania Review: "Black Cherries"

Plainsong: "Light"

Poetry Northwest: "A Basket of Eggs"

Prairie Schooner: "Black Holes," "If I Am Not Real, Then This Is Not Happening," "Silk"

The Southern Poetry Review: "A Shy and New Desire"

Visions: International: "Deathbed, Before"

Willow Springs: "Eulogy for a Suicide"

Zone 3: "Watching from Outside," "The Magician's Desire"

CONTENTS

Prologue

MERRILY, MERRILY, MERRILY, MERRILY

The boat is crowded with translucent figures
who murmur and bump into each other and clink
their oblivious glasses as if they attend
a garden party where peach blossoms
land in their open palms, and no one,
not even the bride-to-be, realizes the doves
already dream of death.
Only the woman with the oars
is real, and she is the only one
who recognizes the other figures and sees
through them to the white-haired woman
asleep in the prow. Her nightmares
skulk along the thwarts. The woman with the oars
bats them away, cursing under her breath:
*you will not die, you will not
die,* but neither this river, nor the willows
along its edge, nor the reflected sky, nor the flat stones
which once skipped across the surface, nor the fish
which feed at the bottom, nor the muck which feeds them,
hears her cry or offers her solace.

I

THE MIDDLE OF THE DAY

The man shovels out a trough, trusting
that the woman sprinkles seeds behind him.
Again this year, he is so determined,
she thinks, so faithful to his hope.
He is imagining the field lacily green
a month hence, he is imagining
wagonloads of food, potatoes that overflow
his hands, pumpkins heavier than his sons.

Tenderness eases into her like mist.
Years later, she will remember her decision
to welcome it, the moment she lifts her face,
nearly surprised at the dry air.
She would like to lay her hand on the damp space
between her husband's oblivious shoulder-blades.
He would believe an angel
had folded one heavy wing
against him; for a moment, he would be still,
offering the angel rest.
She would remove her hand, savoring
his pause, returning it
to her own wistful body.

ROWING TOWARD PINE ISLAND

I strain against the current
in the manner of my father, and the grips
wear against my palms, and the blades
slice through the puddles of sunlight,
and the oar locks clank in their sockets.
The twin cabins recede, flat
against the craggy hill like two wide eyes
chiseled from a stern face. My father marked
his favorite places with weighted milk cartons.
We threw back everything I caught.
You'd better do better than that,
he said, *if you don't want to starve.*
I remembered the photographs, naked children, alone
or clutched against their mothers;
I imagined my belly that big, my picture
in an ad asking my father for money.
He licked his thumb and turned the page.
I baited my own hook.
A generation later, I deny
my blisters, my fiery shoulders. My father,
deserving the rest, will sleep until I return
with enough perch for breakfast.
Now, the oars lie in the green puddle
that laps over my uncomfortable feet
as I drift toward the island's rocky bank.
My pole bobs but the hook flashes
like an empty smile. I'll prove myself
by my forgiveness when he sees my empty hands; I'll know
it's only a joke when he threatens
to give me away.

ANACHRONISM

Like a peasant in a photograph,
the woman enters the pharmacy,
her dark hem drooping
to her calves, her black stockings halted
by shoes as red and startling as two cardinals
settling in a charred wood. Her cane
dark with wear, she is bent
at a perfect right angle and stabs
the floor before her with vehemence
to belie her shuffle. When she juts
her chin out to look up at me,
I expect myself to look away.

Other times from a distance, I have imagined
our conversation, though never
past the point when she reaches
her free hand up to grasp my arm.
I reach into my pocket, hoping
to pull out a red scarf
for her; she would think of me
each morning as she prepared to go out.
But, of course, women haven't worn scarves
in years, and my belief
in miracles is a vestige of childhood.

Her eyes are oily and skittish.
I would not have imagined her skin
so dry beneath the ball of my hand,
my thumb, my fingers suddenly stroking her cheek.
Tracing the line of her jaw, I wonder
whether my trembling is like a mother's

when she remembers, again, how her child
has arisen before her. I restrain my impulse
to glance toward the pharmacist, afraid
his stare will jar my desire
to remain, forever in this place and time.

DEATHBED, AFTER

That this bed stands before a crowd of windows,
the sparrows shrieking for their lives
each morning, the leaves looking like resurrection
before they die,
matters little.

Its metal frame remains,
officious, sanitary,
the sheets laundered and stacked in the closet.
Someone will dismantle
and carry away
this reminder,
as if space in its emptiness
could grow less sad,
as if grief were not liquid enough
to assume the shape
of even an absent container.

ICE AND SNOW, BLESS THE LORD

for Teresinha del'Acqua

Among the twenty nouns Eskimos devote
to snow, two they reserve
for this, the first blizzard of our season,
your life. Such wet silence mutes
the distinction of stem from branch until *tree*
bursts into *fir,* and *fruit* erupts into *cranberry*
or *mistletoe* only within the pleasure
of imagination. As we fling
our arms and legs into wings and gowns,

you teach us *anju*, snow *anju*. We rise
to admire our images, and my breath
hovers at your shoulder, *guardian angel.*
To dispel your fear that snow
would pelt and clatter like hail,
we create our own myths:

We hover among the undiscovered
order of angels whose womanly bodies claim flesh
against the rules. Our leave-takings
transcend grief; we cry
only to celebrate our effervescent pain
defying a blizzard, snow
scalding our cheeks, wind
crystallizing between our lashes.
We live among the undiscovered order
of angels who rejoice so entirely
our bodies arc between our past
and future like gusting snow,

and when none of this is true,
we stand among the coated hedges
and stare into the silent, silent night
where all will still be well.

OBJECTS FOR
STILL LIVES:
THE ORANGE

Even with the smudge pots,
her husband out there all night,
there may be no fruit left.
Each winter she remembers their first harvest,
his thumb splitting the first orange,
proof of wealth to come. Luxury
was the peel curving
around his fist as if he had shaved
away one edge of a spectrum.
This morning, she isn't tempted
to leave him, exactly, but considers
whether he would remember the peel
dropping into her palm, how she twisted
and twisted it between her fingers,
whenever he stroked another's hand.
Surely he would, or does.
He claims to love the ligament
that stretches from her middle finger
when she clenches a pen.
It extends itself even more
when she bends her hand back
to touch the underside of his chin.
Some evenings, she also loves
the look of her hand
more than the texture of his skin.
This morning she loves
his absence. About her odd choices
she's more curious than ever.
What if they raised crocuses

for the saffron?
What if her husband uttered an uncommon word,
luculent or *deciduous*?
She hears him fumble with the silverware,
measuring coffee, before he enters their room.
It's the phrase he whispers too often,
as tenderly as if he sighed her name.
We're saved.

OBJECTS FOR
STILL LIVES:
BLACK CHERRIES

She chooses one cherry
from the bowl, rolls it across her palm,
wishes her skin were as smooth.
Hers feels like the needlepoint on her chair,
an heirloom. Its rough pattern
annoys her. She sits here to teach herself
value in the past. She means to discover
the name for the chunk of history
this chair belongs to.
Above her head, her husband
has hung a painting
of a fish surrounded by the mouth
of an identical but larger fish.
Eating two of the ripest cherries,
she confirms her impression
that she prefers them chilled.
She remembers a trilled voice
revealing the influence
of temperature, texture, color,
as if taste were not an accident
like change. She will remember
this shade after it disappears
into one darker
or light enough to deceive her
into believing in translucence.
She bounces the cherry in her palm.
The needlepoint presses into her back.
In its abstract pattern
she imagines roses, overgrown

and so wild
they collapse into splotches of color.
Her hand twitches as though to scatter
the image into discrete bits of light,
and she turns back
to the bowl on her lap,
the heap of cherries,
each fruit in its own sphere.

OBJECTS FOR
STILL LIVES:
THE PEAR

With one hand he guides
the bottom of the steering wheel,
practicing careless flair;
with the other he grips
the hips of a pear.
Its rough freckles annoy him.
Fruit should fulfill its myth,
frighten him with ripe odor,
gulps of juice.
This pear is so bland
he wants to spit.
He's searching for an orchard keeper
who distills liqueur from the skins
of Bartletts, Kieffers, Garbers.
If he can offer a bottle
with the pear-shaped diamond he's bought
for their anniversary, his wife will believe
his imagination is lively.
She'll believe she should stay.
He hopes the liqueur will taste as full
as her throat. Kissing her there, he wants
no more than to breathe her cologne, a scent as lush
as the wind in July.
He reviews the reasons
she must think him dull:
his insistence on shish kebab every Tuesday,
his collection of fortunes from Chinese dinners,
his ornithologist's life list.
He wishes he still believed

his habits were charming.
Last night when she watered the garden,
he heard her hum an unfamiliar melody.
He can't decide whether the longing
was the song or her voice.
He's certain the slow growth of the eggplant
was all that distracted her.
When he returns
with these bushels of fruit,
his own intuited recipe,
her glance will be happy, startled and happy.

DANCERS AT REST

The eyes on the crucifix stare toward the closed eyes
of the man spread-eagled on the bed, whose live body
is not so finely-detailed. He needs
a shave and a shower, and the woman sleeping beside him
dreams he has both. Because there must be a bird
in every dream, he brings her a canary
in a gold cage she doesn't want.
She shifts her thighs against the heat, and the canary
sprouts tail-feathers of a peacock, all the eyes
as beautiful as the eyes on the porcelain mask
still in its box. He bought it
in order to give her the porcelain ballet slippers
that accompanied it. She didn't believe him
when he said her skin was as beautiful
as the finish, but she fell for him
because he asked her to. He's seen her dance
only a few times, after a few drinks at masquerades.
That's not the chance of fame she abandoned,
if she had one. Her only chance
will be accidental and fleeting: someone else's
foolish picture snapped as she douses herself with the hose,
and flashed across the front page
on the hottest day of the year. It could still happen,
quick as a nightmare, without training or special attire.
If she asked, he'd say he'd take fame
if it fell to him and there was money in it.
He'd dance and drink and eat oysters
and drink for a solid week.
He likes a beer as much as a polka or waltz, but nothing
makes him feel so suave as jazz,
as nothing can persuade her to relax

in a dance hall, with all the drunk and lonely eyes.
He sees an ordinary sky and calls it azure,
an ordinary envelope and calls it alabaster,
and her body droops at the quirks
he mistakes for imagination.
She'd rather risk the generic ambitions
of a bigger apartment, a steady job. Rolling into him,
she grabs a fistful of peacock feathers
which are only his chest hairs, and pulls him awake;
the first thing he sees are her hard
and delicate eyes, her lashes
leaping toward his cry.

FEEDING THE HUNGRY, GIVING DRINK TO THOSE WHO THIRST

*"... I need not feel
grief; I can eat grief..."*
— Sara Suleri, *Meatless Days*

The table is prepared:
the burgundy as robust as blood
coursing through a torso, the crusty bread
uncut and hot, the honey, the butter.

In this gust of time, our lives
seem nearly perfect.
Against the butter knife, the bread board, our touch
is brief and premeditated. Honey floats on my tongue,
a last still point of assurance
before our cascade of grief.

My body hazy with wine, I lean back
into my misbelief that life is
everlasting. We receive the night as a third body
arrived to eat and drink. We've forgotten
how bodies transfuse themselves
into night, first an ordinary
flake of skin, an unmissed eyelash,
then an entire birthmark or scar
twisted among the roots
of a field, soaked up into a tassel of wheat,
kneaded into a loaf
which multiplies as we leave ourselves
at this irresistible edge of hunger,
this brink of thirst.

II

INSOMNIA,
WITH FIREPLACE

That spark is the soul of a crow, that smoke
the breath of the dead. It rises
graceful as a sari, as if the dead still preen
over their bodies. The dead smoke stogies,

play stud poker, keep me
awake, coughing, in the middle of the night. They forget
they're just corpses, courteously decayed. The earth
crushes their lungs. Lichen

blooms along their nerves. They itch
and blame each new rash on the stiff wool
of their funeral suits. They're ready
to teach me the game, dealer calls

aces, deuces, one-eye jacks wild. They drink
Crown Royal from jelly glasses, they eat
cheese and jalapeños. It's New Year's Eve,
it's the Chinese New Year, it's the Eve of St. Swithun.

You're dead, I tell them, dead
and gone, dead and buried, you met your maker,
you're down for the count.
The smoke they blow in my face smells

like frankincense, or so they say. They'll keep me
company, they'll tuck me in with a hot toddy,
they'll tell me a story that ends with marriage.
The dead are obstinate and have no etiquette.

WHAT NO ONE
ELSE KNOWS

Each night she listens
to their hiss as her logs
slouch against the fire. The snow outside
reminds the wood to soften itself
into gray, then white ash. Sparks
rush up her chimney and keep ascending
as if they believe themselves relief
to the North Star, company for Orion. She imagines

him, his denim work shirt nearly frayed,
his belt studded with stars
like some forgotten cowboy, loosening
his hold on the hewn sky and stepping
onto her roof and the roof of her porch
and then with one impossible and graceful
final step, stepping down to her welcome mat.
He pulls against the loose gray handle, unconsciously
lifting her storm door the exact half-inch it asks
to avoid scraping against the warped jamb,
as if he's opened
this door every night through a solid marriage.

When he enters, he's almost ordinary, his hips
thinner than she would have thought, his shoulders more slight.
She would like to rest
her palms against his waist, she would like
to kiss his wrists. If she kisses
the edges of his eyes, the world
they reflect will keep up its agonized spinning
and she will keep breathing, in

and out, sometimes more quickly,
but forever breathing,
if she kisses the bridge of his nose,
if he touches her throat, if he
kisses her ache, her jaw, her face where it aches.

THE TEXTURE
OF SHAME

The wooden back of the scrub brush
feels smooth against his palm,
though it keeps slipping from his grip
and when it does his knuckles scrape
against the sidewalk. His fingers sting,
and his eyes sting from the ricochets
of sun off the white concrete. His mother's black shoes
would be restful against the glare
if they didn't point to the green and blue chalked letters
in his own handwriting. Words
had always been so mysterious, and the peculiar
motions of his tongue had made him want to laugh
until this morning when the girl
revealed these words, squeezing her lips
into a shape like a fish, then spurting
out laughter. Inside his pockets, he twisted
his fingers around the chalk
she'd provided during a flare of generosity.

His mother's shock changed the breeze
against his neck into grit. Her voice
still bangs like a hoe striking a buried stone
in their garden. The sound hurts
his spine and the vibrations in the handle
shoot up his arms. He should have been more careful.
He should have known better
than to take such pleasure in the moist soil
he'd thought was his life.

IF I AM NOT REAL, THEN THIS IS NOT HAPPENING

Knuckled branches startle the moon, as in a Japanese painting.
I could wrap myself around that moon, become circumference
to emptiness in the December sky. I could slide
myself into the silhouette of that kimono, my skin
exchanging molecules with the silk until I have become the silk,
the lotus painted on her sleeve. I could flow into the blue paint
that is a river winding around her waist; I could distill
myself into the black ink representing the blue paint representing
          the river.
I could fold myself up in her hands, insubstantial
as a secret. I could wish myself into the brush
that strokes her hands, one bristle of that brush. But I will not be
the tiny girl in the background, or his hand
grasping the brush, holding her still.

WITH MY HUSBAND

Stroking the arm of the chair
he dozes in all evening
furnishes enough comfort
to spur me through the whole next day.
How lovely he looks,
though we are skittish
of words like *lovely*.

I would like to roll his drink
across his sweating forehead,
but such comfort would disturb him
if only to turn his dream
toward greater comfort,
the lake of his boyhood, our lake,
the lake in his favorite Monet.

By August his forearms are as maple
as the varnish on his chair.
He'll keep it for the roses
carved across the back
until he dies.
He'll cultivate his seven varieties,
cutting a fresh one
for each breakfast table,
until he dies.

By then, he'll have told me how it is
that we can furnish our rooms
with such tenderness,
yet restrain ourselves from touching one another
until one of us is so well asleep.

OBJECTS FOR
STILL LIVES:
A BASKET OF EGGS

It's a child's task,
gathering eggs. The girl enjoys
the pinpricks of light
like stars on the slanted roof of the coop.
She won't touch her hair
until after she scrubs
the dirt and manure from the eggs
and rubs her hands with lotion
that smells like Hawaii.
She knows a home permanent won't make her
any more beautiful, but she hopes
one will make her less shy.
The first time she reached
her shaking hand under a hen,
the hay in the roosts left residue
like pineapple juice on her fingers.
When she wipes the stickiness on her pants,
she ignores the scar
on her second knuckle; its points shrink
when she is warm.
It's not disfigurement
that worries her, but how she will look
or who will live with her
if her face remains so bashful
and her body keeps
giving away her fear.

OBJECTS FOR STILL LIVES: PLUMS

Because the boy wants to cry and doesn't,
his throat feels like he drank cider too hot.
All he sees
through the lighted square
that is the kitchen window
is fruit whizzing past the ceiling fan,
spattering a halo on the wall,
then sliding below his view. *It's plums.*
It's the plums she bought
this morning. He's forgotten
that he's going no farther
than the trash barrel,
that it's too chilly
to be long without a sweater,
that the grass is wet
from the storm all through supper.
His father gestured for the pepper or salt;
his mother nudged the shakers.
The whole night smells like cigarette butts,
coffee grounds, beer cans. Saturday morning,
his mother was sleeping in the easy chair,
her pantyhose bunched on the coffee table.
His father was still gone.
He would go too
if he knew the place
where people threw nothing
but kisses, and he could catch so many
they would clog the spaces between his fingers
if he raised his hand
in the easiest greeting.

OBJECTS FOR
STILL LIVES:
WHITE CANDLES

Her children have scattered spatulas
across the cupboard, searching for the package
of birthday candles to play St. Blase.
She wishes she could stop believing
in blessings; she wishes birthdays
were the only ritual she admitted.
Her husband's fuss over anniversaries,
their carelessly given gifts
are too much lately. Which one
is this — silk? paper? lace? It's as crazy
as he is, keeping track
of martyrs' feast days, refusing surprise
when the vestments are red.
The first time he leaned over her
she felt as if a priest
had touched her throat
with crossed candles. Yet even without him,
she's afraid she would sense a difference
in the weight of the morning.
She wouldn't mind
her husband's flourish
approving the wine's bouquet,
lighting candles whiter than Christ transfigured,
if she didn't recognize his distaste
when he realizes he must still touch her.
She can't claim it's nothing
but respect.
Waiting for any reason
to risk the safety of her soul,
she catches herself
glancing again at the calendar,

assured and disturbed by the dates
printed in red, the feasts, the solemnities,
the ardor of today's memorial.

OBJECTS FOR
STILL LIVES:
APPLES

Each day, he finds an apple
exactly the size of his heart,
one that curves with the curve
of his palm. Bruised ones
tumble by the dozen to his cider press,
but he pockets only the rare
muscular and choice
giants. Seven sit on his window ledge,
absorbing sunlight.
He prefers them as tart
as they would taste the first day,
but cannot bear
to bite into such perfect order;
the most he can do
is whet his paring knife,
testing it against his fingertip.
His heart is the color
of the sides of the apples
away from the streetlight.
He keeps his desk lamp dim,
his dictionary open to the word
sanguineous. He's tried to explain
the pleasure his vision affords,
lights flicking on across the city,
interrupted by these humps of shadow
which could be inside him.
Women decline to meet his eye.
Ripeness filters through his room,
each whiff urging him

to thrust up his window,
lean over the fire escape and juggle
until he's dropped
all but one. That one
he would split in half, perfectly,
to swallow one seed each evening.
When he felt them germinate
in his aorta, he would dare himself
to risk his life.

HABITS OF GRIEF

Back at his dad's is a lake
like this one, hornets buzzing
near the edge, one rowboat
clicking against the dock. My husband
tucks his hands into his pockets. His shoulders slump
under the dusk. His guilt is unwavering,
even as his grief wells and subsides.
Heat lightning makes no promises.

He bows to the water,
glances toward his fishing rod and tackle,
draws back. In an hour, he could catch
a bucket of perch. He hasn't taken the boat out
since his brother jumped from the Huron Bridge,

fourth suicide in this odd family,
each one the one we failed to suspect.
The answer is to leave
what reminds him of childhood, the lakes
he swam across, never winning.
He can't learn to keep
his head down, face in the water.

He turns toward me, and I prepare
my hands to meet his face.
The stubble will be thick,
his collar damp, the lake quiet
behind him wherever I look.
This will never happen
to us, I practice saying, afraid
he doesn't believe it, either.

BATS

My daughter leans her cheek
against my shoulder. Her face
catches what light is cast by the steeple
of a country church on the slope below us.
Watching the sky sink away, she reaches
to pull it back, points to the bats
as graceful and numerous as gulls,
and impossibly white. "Feathers,"

she says, her mouth wet
against my blouse. I don't know
where she's learned the word.
I don't want to correct her. They glide
between the steeple and the silhouette
of a silver birch. I could reach
and pull one down if I were sure she wouldn't
shrink from the silky wings.

Her hair skims my face, chimes
surround us in a hymn
I haven't heard for years, and she stirs.
The shadows are so easy to identify
on a close branch. Her eyelashes
flutter against my thumb,
and I hold her to me,
wondering which of these signals
is turning us slowly towards home.

THE GOOD MORNING

When the boy clicks the latch
as if his whole sleeping family's safety resides
in his cautious departure, he imagines
he's walking into heaven. The sycamore
drops a leaf onto his fishing pole
which the boy understands
is a promise. When he goes
to heaven, he wants it to be
at the time of morning
when the grass is chilly,
when the milkweed pods
begin to split.

The one porch step droops from so many years
of feet. Some days the boy rests
his bare soles there, convinced
that the slope catches extra heat.
Pushing their boat into the lake, he savors
the cold weight the water adds
to his cuffs. They will dry stiff with sand,
the discomfort oddly pleasurable.
He's always wanted this: to be the one
who plans the surprise,
his family waking up
to a special and aromatic breakfast,
and to their awe
that he has risen so early
and waits in his long chef's apron,
calling them.

III

EULOGY FOR A SUICIDE

The woman leans to welcome
her young daughter's kiss.
The girl will never remember this age
when a kiss didn't feel like a noose,

before she dreamt her father was a Minotaur
snorting against her neck.
Her mother said *myth*; others said *story*.
Her father said *Take it back.*

When he lifted his mug and blew
ripples across his coffee, the steam
escaped like a genie while another genie
curled into her mouth, until a whole stream

of genies settled in the space
just above her voice. The choked
feeling roiled like a knot of serpents
she could not cast out. Her mother's jokes

followed her like lies. This afternoon is still
far in the future: her mother leans
storm windows against the fence, taking pleasure
in the peculiar way her reflection careens

into the frames. The glass sparkles,
and so she is unprepared for the bloated
image of an approaching man, the horror
of understanding thrust against her throat.

BLACK HOLES

Today's humidity cloys
like a tongue. Beveled windows
smear the landscape. Memory seeps through, spreads

with sinister will until her throat
welcomes the bitterness and salt, her hands absorb
the pungency. Rolling a ripe olive

across her palm, she drops it
like a promise. Thumbprints mar
the bowl's dark clay. The potter's hand

lurks inside her like a martyr's,
the palm leaning into her brain, the back
backed up against her skull, the stigmata opening

a point of pain. The fetus
was as small as a thumbprint
the night she told him.

With practiced fury, he smashed
his glass and pulled her
against the fireplace, leaving

a black bruise to ring her wrist.
She felt the fetus recoil
into its own zero, heavy

as gravity in its mask of absence.

FINDING THE BODY

The woman hears the thud,
thud of the roofer stomping
above her, like the beat and pause
of a heart. Luminescent and close
to the road, the dogwood drops
its petals. They float like reflections
in the rutted puddle. She won't think
about the horse trailer that scored her yard.

Inside, the stallion was restless and unaccustomed
to confinement. Out back, the mare
huddled against the fence. The colt
would be good for a few hundred,
if money were what she wanted. She wants the garden
plowed under before she can bury
her hands in the wet soil,
searching out radishes and onions. The man
who owned the stallion had struck
a deal with her husband,
who is dead. She knows he is dead
because his wrist feels like clay
and the rim of his lips
is dark, dark as frost
coating a shed snakeskin.

OBJECTS FOR STILL LIVES: A GLASS OF BURGUNDY

This man asks her questions
with three-syllable words. He doesn't instruct her
about her napkin or drink his wine
as though he's afraid
of being caught. When the dessert comes,
when she is filled and happy and he is pleased
that she does not dribble ice cream
onto her collar, he will tell her
he is going to marry her mother.
They act as if they have kept
their secret, which she will keep
for them. She is good
at keeping secrets; she has never told anyone
that her real father left
to buy aspirin and never came back.
He made stained-glass windows
and was killed by a swinging boom
at the new cathedral
is what she tells her friends.
This man's fingers tilt his glass
so his wine sways toward him.
They could never be tense enough
to clench an ax or be clenched.
His name is Richard,
but soon she will call him something else.
This will be the one time
when nothing is just her imagination.

OBJECTS FOR
STILL LIVES:
A WHITE JUG AND
LARGE WHITE BOWL

The jug is as white as the one
Christ chose, washing their feet.
She wants to fill it with milk,
and the bowl with rice, set them both
on a white linen tablecloth
between two mirrors. Like a boy
spotting Saturn through his first telescope,
her husband will be stunned and afraid and understand
that infinity is more
than mathematics. The slight
tremor in his hands will disrupt
the buffer of electrons between their bodies
just enough to make his hesitancy
her hesitancy too. Then a jay
will screech to its mate, and their throats
will clench the endearments they've refused
like a fist clenching that bird.
When he grabs her wrist,
her buttons will dent her skin
along the lines her mother called
the nerve of tenderness
and the nerve of abandonment.
She will remember him
by the twist of dark hair
against his stiff collar as he leaves,
and by her wish
that she had left
well enough alone —
these museum pieces on their corner table
where they have been displayed, properly, all these years.

OBJECTS FOR STILL LIVES: LIGHT

It's long into night when she lights
the wick of her oil lamp,
keeping the flame low, sitting
so one side of her face
remains invisible. When her husband
urged her to imagine
his hand in whatever light
wavered across her face, she assumed
he meant to stay.
Everything recalls her startled pain
catching the reflection
of sun and lake off his canoe.
Then he brought her perch and bluegills
whose shade shifted
according to their angle in her hands.
She attends to how differently
light passes through
condensation on a mug,
the slant of its handle.
The radio's gleam strikes her cheek.
Grateful that some element absorbs light
and grows heavier for it,
she drinks often from stoneware
and has begun to feel solid
late in the day. The solution
is simpler than time. When she's the nerve
she will switch on every lamp,
ignite the Coleman lantern,
string Christmas bulbs across the garage,
sicken herself with memory
until light is reminiscent only of light.

THE DEAD WHO
ARE NOT RAISED

Her life drawing instructor insisted
she visit the Museum of Natural History,
spend a morning before an open sarcophagus,
sketching. The mummy she chooses
had been a woman; someone has removed
the blackened linen strips from her right foreleg,
her hands, her face. Someone has x-rayed
her torso, and someone has printed labels
with arrows pointing to her ribs, her hips
as if in response: yes,
she was a woman.

The labels describe cycles of famine,
ceremonies of burial.
None mentions the guardianship
of the dead woman's mother and lover,
their ache of powerlessness
either to cleanse their grief here
or to forgive the spectators. The woman's spirit
leans above and into the body, face pressing against face,
thigh against thigh, breast against breast.

The student forces her eyes toward the closed eyes,
the tight lids, gaping
follicles, the stretched skin pulling lips
away from teeth, black curves
bounding incisors and jaw.

The small open hands seem to have relinquished
their agony, and the student feels her voyeurism
nearly forgiven, and she nearly believes
they gesture in welcome.

She could begin with these hands
in repose; the charcoal fits itself
against her fingertips as she prepares
to disregard the tibia
jutting through the leg's split skin, the rigid black
layers of muscle insisting on the body's
opaque and private right
to decay.

THE MAGICIAN'S DESIRE

Disbelieving magic, I've settled my interest
in tricks. My appearance on-stage
has grown so perfect, my flourished gestures
so refined, I've discarded all mirrors
but this storefront window.
Its marked cards and bottomless glasses
make my sort of life look easy.

The face I've vowed to forget
emerges from my reflection, repeating
You are not a part of our family.
I saunter on, so unbetrayed
by my own face that some accuse me
of one happy-go-lucky day after another.

If everything is silver and glittery,
if children love the parents who bring them,
my act is not just a trick.
Anyone's appearance can be changed
with brighter light, a double black curtain.
Parakeets and bouquets disappear each evening.
Then I go, as tradition
would have it, in a puff of smoke,
turning up after a minute of applause
for an encore, a final bow.

When I disappear the final time,
wishing it were the final time,
the chairs scrape back
and I hear the voices gathering their groups,
their families. The lovers grab hold

of each other; one couple
catches my glance. The man's hand
glides down the woman's back,
so content to be
slower than my eye.

WHERE PEOPLE GO
WHEN THEY DIE

The child settles her chin
on the windowsill and looks into the dark sky
for her father, who is an angel
and lives on the moon.
White squirrels make him grin, and white horses
gallop through the white sand. The full moon
is a beach without water, and the crescent moon
is a beach when the water comes back.
The angels who live there are all too lonely
for swimming. When her father is thirsty
for lemonade or a beer, he waits
until night and flies back
to their kitchen. His wings light up
their house; they feel like her mother's scarves
when he curls them around her dreaming body.

WATCHING FROM OUTSIDE

The wooden steps are cluttered with chips
of white paint that have flaked from the shutters
since last winter. Through the screen, I can see
flour softening the air,
my grandmother rolling dough,
cutting a circle in quick, short strokes
for the top crust. An apple peel spirals
toward a heap of white cores near the fork
she lifts to press the crusts together
in the perfectly ordered lines I will always love
like the perfect stillness of her kitchen the moment before
my hand clatters the wooden door against its wooden frame.

DUSK ON THE LAKE

My father's back is sloped
like the hill across the lake
as he sits alone on the dock.
In a few hours, he will carry his pail
to the wooden table behind our cabin,
where he will scale a dozen bluegills and perch.
Tomorrow night, I will fry them with potatoes and onions.

He doesn't know I watch him.
He doesn't know I also see my mother
alone in the front room
when his faded blue shirt matches the dusk.
The porch swing squeaks from a gust off the lake.
I shiver without a sweater, but I am afraid
the moment I go, my father will turn
to beckon me toward him, to offer
his rod and reel, a can of bait, hints on casting.
I envy the way his wrist swings behind his head
just before the sinker makes a small splash
far from the dock.
His arm is tan below his rolled shirt sleeve.
My arm is curled around the post
on the corner of our porch,
and all I wish is that I did not know
this is the most we will ever have.

IV

A SHY AND NEW DESIRE

Her fingers spread wide, the woman sinks
her hands into the soil, easy
from the spade and rake. She plants peppers
for herself, carrots for her lover.
Within a week, fronds will brush through, tentative, and soft
as eyelashes. She starts at her memory,
her lover's body
matched against her own, a globe
of white glass hung in her stomach
until her lover's hand rests
against her, and the glass explodes, a burst prism,
magenta and orchid and cobalt spilling

from her body. Her impulse
to lie down, to stretch herself out, her stomach leaning
into the soil as water
leans into a cupped hand,
astonishes her. A few weeks longer, and the first orange root
will shrug into light, sheepish as a grin,
sloped as a shoulder
she leans to kiss.

SPONGE BATH

Most of the women adjust
their wigs and blankets and worry
that I'll notice
they're still not as beautiful
as their husbands claimed.
One believes I am
her husband. One never
embraced a husband. She asks
Who are you?
I don't know you.
I say my name once
or twice or until she believes
I'm permitted to touch her.

I am afraid
my hands will feel as abrasive
as the brisk slaps
she remembers each week
as if her father still lurked in the hall.
Her lilac soap recalls
her mother's welcome.
You're not my mother, are you?
I say my name again, slipping
a towel around her shoulders.
My mother died, didn't she?
Yes, I say, *and your father died, too.*

I'm not like my father.
Did my children die? she asks once.
You had no children, I say;
you never married.
Did I hurt my children?

No, and when I sigh, my breath
lurches like a punch. When she is clean
and comfortable, I promise
as always to return. *Don't,*
she says, *be afraid.*

TAKING LEAVE

We agree the open-air market has lost its charm,
but I stop this morning
because I grew enamored of it
the summer we grew enamored
of each other, and because you love
succulence, surprises you can call exotic,
fresh pineapple for breakfast,
and because I am about to be cruel.

I set our plates
on the patio, our coffee cups, our juice.
The eggs can simmer
until you emerge, expectant and damp.
You'll see the pineapple in its own bowl
and think this treat a prelude
to a whole day of modest blessings.

I would have this moment
stretch itself out like a trumpet's whine,
uneasy and safe from talk.

What I want isn't so much,
is so slight and unforgivable —
a new window to look out of,
a new bed, a new garden,
a new window to look out of.

S I L K

I slide my hand into the sleeve —
such translucent burgundy, such light pressure —
and longing catches me off guard,
rising more quickly than memory
into my thighs, shoulders, throat.

I almost see him
at the mirror, knotting his tie,
his final satisfied tug my favorite gesture.
His reflection interrupts
the confused reflection of our bed, the sheets
still rumpled from our leisurely
arousal. My slip lingers against my waist
like a hand, until I stretch
to kiss the stray black hairs of his nape, my arms
crossed over his chest, my breasts
resting through the thin fabric
against his firm back.

It did happen once,
or twice, but more often I checked the impulse
to lean into him, afraid
of his shrug. Now, when I gaze
into the mirror, it's the dip in my own throat
I see, the low, open V of my blouse,
as I attend to the cool solace
of fabric against the curve of my underarm
as if touch alone could satisfy such startling desire.

THE PHARAOH'S SERVANT

As the first man entered our tomb,
his beard was like flecks of rust
and the sun quivered against his right shoulder.
His dialect was as soothing as aloe.
I wanted to inhale syllables I couldn't understand,
syllables he repeated
almost slowly enough for me to remember
before he stepped away.
His shoes were brown cloth.
I watched the sand settle in his tracks.

I knew he was ignorant of my vows to remain
and would sacrifice them
for knowledge, would take me,
my grain and bracelets and the baskets I had woven
before my wedding,
to Cairo, as once I had sacrificed my body
for the knowledge of what comes later.

Nothing comes later.
I was hungry; I was tired.
My body was heavy, and so I slept
until a young man
lifted my arm, turned my face.
Most of my hair was gone.
My skin had split
like linen over a razor.
I had expected something different.

Bodies probe the crevices of mine,
count my teeth,
measure my brain.
I hear scholars
debate my belief in a resurrection
greater than a portrait on stiff paper.
During their arguments, I almost believe
knowledge enough equals immortality,
that hope they can't deny.

DEATHBED, BEFORE

She can see the criss-crosses of sunlight
on her mother's kitchen table
Sunday mornings. She'd sung a hymn
whose tempo matched the flickering curtain,
a hymn she would sing like a blessing
over the rising dough.

The taste of lemon at the back of her tongue
surprises her more than her loss
of feeling. As a girl she'd held
a coin out to the baker,
who'd replaced it with a lemon tart.
Its crust was perfectly pleated,
its flavor thrilling as a secret.

Her body shelters its own secrets —
how to disappear, how to be so still
even its future remains undisturbed.

THE OLDE WORLD CAFE

From a second-story window across the street,
a woman with a face as stiff as mine
drops burning papers, letters
she's determined to forget. One man
heckles her from the sidewalk; others laugh
or applaud. She fails to look triumphant.
My husband has gone
to the bar for another carafe of spiced wine.
The woman hesitates as she lifts
the last sheet, the signature
curling back on itself. The long sounds
of his name reverberate
after the last match scrapes into flame.
My husband returns and proposes
a toast to alcohol, autumn,
this restaurant, once our favorite.
Already, she knows she'll take him back
when he phones next week
to complain he's lost
a shirt; could it be at her place?
My husband's shirt was as soft as lint
when I last touched it. This afternoon,
fingering the cuffs and collar, he lays odds
that I'll bluff spunk and forgive him
anything for a promise, as he leans to ask
how I've been.

ABOVE EARTH'S LAMENTATION

Again, we cross over
this bridge so far above its river
I can only think
the word *abyss*.
Mist thickens through the gorge
until the river
becomes an act of faith.
I have read of the time when God
had not yet separated
the waters above the sky
from the waters below the sky,

and all the separations after,
I came to bring division already begun.
I cannot count
the separations which have raised me up,
can only begin: male, female.

I meant to remain awed
by the creation
of light, darkness, earth, sea, sky,
but there it is: male, female

and memory
of the man who claimed
women reflect men; men reflect God.

In my anger I did not argue.
After betrayal enough, leaving
grows easy, turning away

becomes a blessing, as the earth
blesses itself in its persistent rotation.
My woman's body is reconcilable
only to another's:
eyelids, lips, breasts:
my incarnate longing.

A BLESSING FOR
THE NEIGHBORHOOD

I'm carrying in the last sack
when Kim asks to help.
Yes is easy this time.
She lugs the milk like a watermelon
she can't wait to break into,
like an offer of a life that luscious.

She settles for a ride on my shoulders
later. I jog between chunks of sidewalk
as if risk measured precisely
would save us all. A drunk
directs traffic on the corner, and Kim
gleefully reveals why two women
loiter under the streetlight.

Lifting her down, I kiss
the shell of her ear.
Kiss me again, she says, so I do.
She presses her ear against mine
until we hear the ocean,
the waves breaking between us.

A voice calls her in, and I go in.
When I look out, my own disembodied face
stares blankly back; then Kim is behind it,
skipping up the sidewalk, stumbling, catching herself
as if the easiest trick
is to shun the world's embrace.

THE UNDERTAKER
LEAVES WITH YOUR BODY

I'd never thought about body bags
apart from war and wish I did not remember
the gray vinyl, the zipper, as ordinary
as cheap luggage, assuming the form
of your corpse.
Days before we'd still been counting
your breaths, one every twenty seconds,
every thirty. Oiled crosses shone
on the backs of your hands, last sacrament —
in those days every event the last
of its kind.

In your casket you looked simply relieved,
and I was grateful for the reverence
of the man who had prepared your body,
the prescribed order of ritual,
the dignity of wood which burns
like memory
and is never consumed.

L A U D S

How early you're awake,
sipping your coffee
on the porch. The land slopes
with the same curve
as the well of your cup
fitted perfectly against your palm.
Gusts look almost like rain
over the lake. Someone will know
what to call the two trees
flowering at its edge and the duck
that is not the mallard.
You mull over possibilities
beyond species or family.

Out front, goldfish swerve
through the base of the fountain;
you remember your surprise
at the albinos. Past them, buds
exhale, opening into their names.

But how usual is this part
you savor, the urgency back here
of everything you've seen before,
hill and *twig* and *white* and *breeze,*
calling you so suddenly to utter them.

THE LAST
CORPORAL WORK

I chant alleluia but I will not say amen.
To hell with sacrilege. I could conjure up
an image of Jesus and lock my arms
around his skinny legs and beg. And every damn time
he laughs his embarrassed laugh, as human
and unmoved as the rest, and pries my hands away.
And so I dream I have lain down
beside you, and my favor is so quiet
you almost can't hear: *don't die, don't die.* My belief
is senseless, that anything would be different
if I had grabbed hold of the soil, prodigal black handfuls
before that objective and ominous machine
had pressed it back upon you.
In the midst of our long procession leaving
the cemetery, I stared only ahead, my hands cupped open,
empty and heavy with liturgy. Solace
is an invention of the indifferent. Your god
rattles off his stories.
Breathing his last, he says *it is finished.*
It is never finished.

LUCIFER'S DEFEAT

The first illusion was of success,
of surfing across the still
unseparated waters, of a body
as indefatigable as the breeze.

I felt my hips falling
into more of myself
like the Ohio, which didn't yet spill, spilling
into the Mississippi.

My lips opened into an ellipse, savoring
the prospect of a first season's first
strawberry, which hadn't yet ripened
or blossomed or germinated in a musky furrow,

which did exist
in my mind. I already loved land,
fertile or not, clay as well as humus; I even loved
relief maps with their ridges and whorls, their indentations

tempting my fingers to rest
in their crevices, to trace
the edges of blue that would be
lakes after the glaciers

I already imagined, to probe
canyons and coves as if I did
hold the world in the palm of my hand.
I could hold some of it,

clusters of cells skimmed from the Ganges,
fistfuls of amoeba, bacteria
which would become tropical
ferns beside coconut and papaya and mango,

or would migrate to the Australian outback
and rise up generations later as thistle or sage,
or would remain aquatic to become
an air sac or carapace or adipose fin

which would all lead to hooves and hair
and shoulders, to mammals and then men
and women. With time enough, I could touch
an atom in each of its forms —

feather, coal, exhaled breath. But the world, no —
I could not hold it all.

FOR THEY SHALL
BE COMFORTED

Muscular and ignorant of pain,
the corpse lunges forward; the cross is lost
in this ancient altar piece
among flourishes of technique.

No women mourn at the foot of this cross;
no friend claims the body.
Whispering tourists pass into the next hall.
I rest in a pew carved *circa 1580*.

With days yet to die, how could your body
have looked so like a corpse? How could this Christ
have been imagined so unscathed?
The one stained window relieves my rage,

each pane an illustration of ancestry,
each figure leading ineluctably toward crucifixion.
A shoot sprouts in this art
from the stump of Jesse, and climbs

through the pane of Abraham, the pane of David,
the pane of Mary. A segment of blue light
falls from her sleeve and would pierce my hand,
as a shaft of yellow light always connects her

to the angel who comes with his peculiar greeting.
When I turn my hand over, the blue settles
with the cool weight of a small stone
in my palm, until I fold my hand around it

and it becomes a breath breathed into my skin,
a breath I can exhale, as if what makes us living beings
were not the breath of God,
but our release of it.

LYNN DOMINA was born and grew up in and around Saginaw, Michigan. She earned a B.A. at Michigan State University and an M.F.A. at The University of Alabama, where she received an Academy of American Poets Prize and edited *The Black Warrior Review*. She is currently living on Long Island and completing a Ph.D. in American literature at The State University of New York at Stony Brook.